T0194628

Overcoming
the
Barricades *of* Life

Brian D'Alo

WESTBOW
PRESS®
A DIVISION OF THOMAS NELSON
& ZONDERVAN

WestBow Press books may be ordered through booksellers or by contacting:

WestBow Press
A Division of Thomas Nelson & Zondervan
1663 Liberty Drive
Bloomington, IN 47403
www.westbowpress.com
1 (866) 928-1240

ISBN: 978-1-9736-6247-1 (sc)
ISBN: 978-1-9736-6242-6 (e)

Print information available on the last page.

WestBow Press rev. date: 05/07/2019

I dedicate this book to my wonderful wife and my fantastic children for their love and support in all my endeavors in life. I thank God every day for them.

Introduction

YOU HAVE TAKEN A big step towards trying to overcome barriers and blockades in your life between yourself and where you want to be in life. You have recognized a very important, and sometimes very troublesome truth in your life. But what is it? Take a moment to think about it. The truth that this book is about is that we have things that stand in the way of ourselves and possibly others from achieving what we or they want in life. Whether that be happiness, love, a relationship with those around us, or a relationship with God. The core of this truth is that these barricades and these obstacles are in our path and around us by someone whom we would not suspect at first because it's usually a very uncomfortable thing to see. We put these things where they are by ourselves. The most interesting part of this truth is that in finding, placing, and sometimes fortifying what becomes a barricade between us and these things we want, we are all lifetime experts. This book is an exploration of this subject by doing a study in the Bible of the Book of Jonah in relation to this topic.

Now before we begin, allow me to introduce myself. I am not one that has any special training or certifications or degrees in religious or self-help areas of study. I am as "broken" as they come in many areas that God has revealed while writing this book and discussing its topic with those around me. I am a computer repair expert and part-time author. I don't write as a profession, however; this is one book that God has laid on my heart as I have thought about this topic it would be a topic of great worth to write about and to you to read about and to take what you read and apply it to life to improve your life but also to help you have better relationships with those around you, and to have a better relationship with the Lord.

Now to help you understand that I am a normal person like you, let me tell you a little about where I stand at the writing of this book. I am a happily married person with a wonderful wife and two wonderful children. Or at least that is what you would see from the outside. From the inside, yes I am happily married and hope, that my wife would say the same. Now for my kids, the relationship I have with them is where there are major barriers and obstacles, caused by myself and the happenings of the events of my growing up in what most would characterize as either a non-Christian or barely Christian home based on the teachings of Christ-like behavior and Godly lifestyle. Yes, there were quite a few teachings about who God and His Son, Jesus Christ, are, however; there was nothing about trying to have a true relationship with them. This was a foreign and an uncomfortable concept for me to wrestle with for quite a while and was quite the obstacle to overcome. The events that occurred while I was growing up caused me to create so many barricades and obstacles around me it has taken years to overcome a few, and the rest of them create a virtual minefield for anyone that dares to come in close.

That's where this study of Jonah has come into my life. Seeing and learning and applying the lessons we will delve into in this book are part of what has helped me, unknowingly until God revealed it while I was attending a men's retreat in the desert in California one weekend, to overcome things that had been in my way of happiness in life in both the temporal and the spiritual senses of the word.

Now I ask that you take a moment before starting to the main portion of this book, take a moment to clear your mind and center yourself before God now and each time you read, so He might speak to your heart and show you what you need to know from this book. He will have things to show you about yourself, and also about your relationships with others around you. Allow God to show you what He has for you in this study.

T O BEGIN THIS TRIP we first need to know a little about who and what this is all about. Who was Jonah? Why is he important? What was so special about him that made them include him in the Bible, to begin with? What can we learn from a general reading of his story? Most people glance over the entire book of Jonah while others read different things about it as being a story about being obedient to God's commands and instructions. While this is an important lesson we will touch on, there is so much more inside this book we can learn.

They describe Jonah as being a Prophet. Now ask yourself, what does this mean to you? What is a Prophet? Why is this an important thing to know and understand? Does this even matter? In small ways it does. It takes a lot of patience sometimes to go through history and to get the background but this time it will take things a deeper understanding.

Brian D'Alo

First, what is a Prophet? The biblical meaning of it is someone who has received a message from God and He then commands this person to bring that message to God's people. The more general meaning is that a Prophet is God's mouthpiece to mankind. This is significant because having a living God who cares for His people to the point of giving His people someone who can tell all of them exactly what He wants them to do. God gave Jonah a specific message just like other Prophets before him. Most of the time these were messages that told to people to repent and turn away from sin and turn back to God. Other times they were warnings meant to aid them in their spiritual walk of life.

Now, what does his having been a Prophet mean for you? This means that Jonah was someone to pay attention to not only in his time but today. God had chosen and anointed him to be His mouthpiece to the people of the world. They wrote what God told them to and what happened to them, not only for the people of their time but also for us today. With that calling, we should pay attention to all that the messages that the Bible offers us today. The larger message of obedience and the other smaller, yet very important, messages are for all ages and are timeless and necessary for our lives today.

The story of Jonah has been one that has influenced countless people over the years. It's influenced people from its literal interpretation and figurative interpretations. Interpreting it in the literal sense when misfortune came to a naval voyage some sailors thought it was because of disobedience to God's commands. They would find the "Jonah" among them and make sure they righted whatever the evil deed was, even up to the person being thrown overboard how Jonah was. The person usually agreed that they caused God's anger with them and was why they had lost their wind, weren't catching anything they were out to catch, etc.

Now, what does this mean? This is part of the literal meaning that people take from the Book of Jonah. That there are physical barriers and obstacles brought into our lives as we are disobedient to God's commands that will affect us and those around us. What kinds of barriers and obstacles have you seen in your life and have blamed on either God or blamed yourself or someone else for causing them in your life? We will go into greater depth on these types of barriers and obstacles later on in this book.

As for the figurative lessons, every time someone reads it they come away with a new lesson or a new insight they can apply to their spiritual life. This is the wonderful nature of the Bible, it allows God to speak to us according to our individual points in life and teach us, and slap us in the face, with the truths He wants and needs us to have just like those prophets of old did during the Biblical times. This is true whether you belong to a religion that believes in modern-day prophets or that they are a tool that God used only in biblical times.

There are simple lessons on the surface for all to see and read and learn in the Book of Jonah and there are deeper ones that hit on a different level of physical and emotional and spiritual understanding. We will look at these different aspects of the Book while we embark on this study. We hope and pray that you will approach this as not just another study to check off a list saying OK this is one more done. Don't just read through this book in one sitting and then place it back on the shelf. Take the time to read through this a portion at a time and prayerfully approach each portion of this with the intent on letting God speak to you and enter your heart and life to help you change whatever He is leading you to see and feel the desire or need to change.

That is our goal in this, to help everyone who truly wants to read and study and prayerfully submits to God to have Him work inside, that they will gain a closer relationship with God and His Son and gain a better understanding of the roles we play for ourselves and for others we come into contact with.

Let start in the best place we can to study this book, chapter 1 verse 1 of the Book of Jonah. This is a short book in the Bible being only four chapters long. The beginning of the book is where Jonah gets his call from The Lord to go to the people of Nineveh and to preach to them. God said the reason that Jonah was being sent there was that the people of Nineveh were wicked. Nineveh was a rough place to live and getting the call to go there and to preach would be like one of us being told by God to go to the most iniquitous city you can picture that has the roughest and most sinful people you can imagine. Now you can imagine that Jonah was probably worried or scared about this task given him. Can you blame Jonah for succumbing to his human tendencies and running away?

He would run to Tarshish to run away from God. How often does running cause us problems in life? We try to run from one problem and it tends to either rear its head at us from a different angle or it steers us into a bigger problem. Instead of turning to God and trusting Him in our problems, we cause bigger and worse ones for ourselves. God was willing to aide Jonah in his task anyway he asked because of his nature of being a prophet of God. Think of how willing God is to assist us as His children. Why run from problems when you have God on your side willing and able to help you. We have our tendencies to puff out our chest and take these problems on ourselves. Yes, we can be strong, however; that is not why that obstacle is there. It is not there for us to show how strong we can be. It is there as something to tell you that during your God-given task, whatever it may be, He is there to help and assist but only if you seek Him out during the problem times.

Jonah did not do this, he faltered he wavered in his faith just enough to allow fear inside and to set his feet moving in the opposite direction of Nineveh. He got to Joppa, and this is where our naval friends get their Jonah related beliefs regarding great storms and bad luck at sea. Jonah boards a boat to get him to Tarshish and once the boat sets sail, God causes an obstacle to arise for the entire crew and every passenger. Most people have this mental image at this point of the story it is just Jonah and the crew, maybe a captain and a handful of crewmen to make sure the rigging was good for the sails, or maybe a few rowers for them to propel themselves across the waters to Tarshish. These were business people who were running this ship. Either Jonah was lucky and got a cheap cruise on a small fishing boat or this was a regular ferry style ship. In which case, there were more people on board who were fearing for their lives and worrying about their families. They would want to know the cause of the storm that suddenly rose around them. Put yourself in their shoes. You are on board that ship heading off on a trip with your family. You boarded the ship to cross the sea and then when the ship casts off and you are near the middle of your journey; the wind picks up and slams waves against the side of the ship. The other passengers are screaming and are pleading with the crew to keep them safe. They do everything they can to keep the ship from capsizing and they realize that this storm could have only have come from a source other than nature.

They search for that cause among themselves, however; when they cannot find it they resort to casting lots to determine who was at fault. They would usually roll dice, such as they were, believing that the dice would reveal the will of God or some other supernatural power. They decided that whoever the lot fell on would be the one that was the problem. The lot fell on Jonah who, after being questioned, confessed what he had done. This is the hardest thing someone can do, admit that they did something wrong. We all have had to do this at some point, probably within the last few hours even. Think about how you felt when you last had to admit that you were wrong or had done something wrong. It probably made you want to throw up walls to stop those around you from hurting you either emotionally and physically even though you may have known that there was no harm coming. Now here is the question we should ask. How should we react to the truth being exposed in a situation when it means that it can or will hurt us? What does the bible and God teach us on this matter? Jonah teaches us a great lesson on this when he gets "found out."

He doesn't shirk his responsibility for having caused this storm from happening. He doesn't run away from the problem this time. He accepts responsibility for what is happening and he, in fact, tells them exactly what is going on, why it is going on and what they need to do to save themselves. This is the mark of a prophet and messenger of God what they are to be doing and saying to the people they are to be ministering to. His concern is for the salvation of those around him. Here we are seeing Jonah changing his heart from how it had been when he had gotten onto that ship. He tells them I want you to believe and to do that he tells them to throw him overboard so they would be saved from the storm. Now put yourself into the shoes of the sailors on the ship. They probably thought he was crazy. They didn't want to do it; they knew what happens if you fall overboard on the sea in a storm. You go into that water; they knew he wouldn't be coming out. They kept rowing for land; they didn't want to have Jonah's life on their hands, however; they made no headway. It finally came down to a very difficult decision for them to make. Either they throw Jonah into the water, or they all die for the sins of one person.

We come across this often in our spiritual life. We have that one friend or group of friends that live their lives in such a way that when we associate with them; it causes a spiritual storm in our life. The longer we are with them the stronger the storm gets. It comes to a point where we need to make the decision that those sailors made. Do we go down with the ship of iniquity and allow that spiritual storm to drown us, or do we follow God and cast the iniquity and the thing that is an evil or something that God has told or warned us we are not to have or do overboard and away from us so we can be saved and remain close to God and improve our walk with Him?

The sailors had a difficult choice to make. What choice would you have made? Would you have thrown Jonah into the water, or would you have kept him on board and tried something else to save yourself, the ship and the rest of the people onboard? The sailors choice was to follow the instructions from God's servant. They first said a prayer and told God they would do this because we believe that You want us to. They followed that up by still asking that Jonah's blood would not be on their hands. They then took Jonah and threw him into the water. Even after having prayed and asked God not to punish them for doing this deed, they still performed the required sacrifices and vows to attain forgiveness for their sins. This is something we can learn a great lesson to remain close to God. The Bible says nothing that is unclean can be with God. These sailors made sure they were spiritually clean before God. We need to do the same thing. If we suspect that we have sinned, while the sacrifice of Jesus Christ has atoned for our sins, we still need to humble ourselves before God and ask for forgiveness and then make the required changes in our lives to align our lives to make sure we are having a closer walk with God.

These sailors saw the blessing of having done these things pretty much right away. The storm ceased raging around them. The waves calmed, the winds stopped. Imagine this happening around you. You've turned the helm of the ship of your life over to The Lord and turned away from that sinful place you were in or headed to. You threw that person or cargo that was causing the storm in your life overboard into the sea and repented of your sins. Then the clouds break and the sun shines on you again. Its warm rays wash over you as the waves stop crashing against your hull and all you hear is the calming slosh of the water as the ship calmly cuts its way through the sea of life and the world. This would be an amazing sight and feeling, would it not? You can have that feeling all the time if you allow it as those sailors did.

Jonah had more trials ahead of him, just like we inevitably all do in our lives. He first had to have his iniquitous old self die, and he needed to put away those behaviors and ways of thinking. This is what his being thrown into the sea was. It was a symbol of the death and burial of the old self. However, just being thrown into the water would have caused actual death and the symbolic one. To avoid this, God had prepared a great fish to swallow up Jonah so that Jonah would live. This was not a short visit inside of this fish either. Jonah was in that fish for three days. He spent that time crying out to God. He laid it all out before The Lord, everything on and in his heart, Jonah put it on the table and said God I messed up but it's time to change me and break down this wall I tried to put up between us. He changed and said I will do what You want me to. God heard Jonah and caused the fish to put Jonah back onto dry land. Not in the best and cleanest way though.

God had the fish vomit Jonah onto the shore. God made sure that Jonah would have a lasting reminder about what had just happened. Think about what this experience would do to you. You survived a terrible storm, but only by being thrown into the water. You lived inside a fish for three days. Then the fish regurgitated you onto the shore. This would be a firm, lasting impression. You would remember this experience for the rest of your life. I know that God has done this with me many times. God has made sure that certain things remain with me so I am reminded of things I should do and that I definitely should not do. It also serves as a reminder to us that it is upon God that we must rely upon for our strength to do what He wants us to do because it is a reminder to us of how He is bigger and stronger than us. Jonah needed this reminder at this point and he surely got that reminder, with a side order of whatever partially digested lunch that great fish had that day.

So what does Jonah do after this experience? Does he lollygag around and ponder the meaning of life? Does he sit and moan about his situation? Or does he get up and move? He gets up, and he goes to Nineveh. He was probably still afraid of what the people would do to him but with a newfound confidence that God has his back and would protect him. And with this confidence, Jonah delivers his message while still expecting the people of Nineveh to act as they had historically done. He expects them to reject the message and as a result; he expects them to have God's wrath come down on them. That was the message that God had sent Jonah to Nineveh to deliver. Repent or experience the wrath of God and watch as it utterly destroys the surrounding city and the inhabitants along with it. The people believed his message and repented. The message hit home with the ruler of Nineveh and he repented of his wickedness. He then told all the people of the city to do the same. Meanwhile, what was Jonah doing? He was angrily setting up a nice spot on the sidelines of the city to bemoan his fate.

I can imagine it with a slightly modern flair. He's sitting on a cliff overlooking the city in his folding lawn chair with his head in his hands saying "oh woe is me." Now it wasn't a pleasant, comfortable day that day. The sun was shining, and it was hot. Jonah probably was physically miserable and sweating while watching the events around Nineveh and seeing these people repenting and turning to God. Now God knew what was going on with Jonah, so He provided shade for Jonah to help comfort him. He caused a tree to grow right next to Jonah. This probably helped ease some of his physical discomforts. It thrilled Jonah to have this tree there. Now Jonah was not very appreciative of God in this miraculous tree. He appreciated the tree and the comfort it allowed him but he didn't appreciate God and His providing to Jonah of this comfort. So what does God do? He makes the tree shrivel and die. Once again God is teaching Jonah a lesson. He is teaching Jonah, and us, that He is in control of all things. How often do we forget this? God is in control in our lives in so many ways, even the small, simple, and mundane ways. We love to be in control of everything in our lives and enjoy the blessings we get, but how often do we give God the praise and glory for having provided and given us these things?

God reminds him that our fates and future are in His hands and that He sees and knows all that all of us do. Including the people of Nineveh who needed to have this reminder about how to behave and to go about their temporal and spiritual lives by God's messenger and told by His messenger, they needed to turn from their wicked ways and turn to God. The people of Nineveh overcame a major barrier between themselves and their life and walk with God. Now let's shift over to thinking about us and our lives for a moment. Do we have barriers in our lives we have created by our actions? Do we have barricades created because we want to continue doing certain things even when God has told us through one of his many messengers to turn away from that behavior? What stands between us and God by our conscious design? What blocks us from the fullness of His love by our subconscious designs?

Let's look now at the barricades one by one that Jonah tried to erect to block out what he didn't want to have happen to him. He really did not want to go to Nineveh. He probably wanted to go somewhere where all would welcome him and life would be easy. Imagine it, would you want to go to an easy or a difficult and possibly dangerous mission field? Would you take the easy path of least resistance? Would you take the path that leads into hard times? Would you accept nearly certain pain and heartache? I think I can imagine your answer. We all would prefer the safe, easy one. I would prefer the safe and easy path every time someone presents it.

However, this is not what God wanted or needed from Jonah. He told him to go where Jonah's particular talents and skills were in the greatest demand. God was sending him to where Jonah was needed and where he could share God's blessings and message, not just for Nineveh's benefit but for also for Jonah's benefit. That is the key to remember. Whenever God calls us to do a certain ministry or task, He designs it to benefit certain people or groups of people and to glorify Him. God knows everything we will do when He gives us a task or a ministry. He knows where you will succeed and where the failures will occur. Think about that for a moment. He knew that Jonah would falter and run away. He knows where we will falter and run away. Where are we trying to run away from God in our lives? Is it in a particular ministry? Has He called us to go to a certain area in the world or in our community to serve Him by bringing them His message? Has it been in our personal lives and relationships? Are we seeking His will in our relationships? What about our finances? Have we tried running away from being prompted and told through biblical teaching to offer our tithes and offerings?

Jonah tried to put a large distance between himself and where God wanted him to be. He boarded that boat heading to Tarshish and then he would go who knows where else in his attempt to hide. He even went below decks into the cabin area and slept, trying to stay out of God's sight. He faltered in his faith that God would protect and provide for him and instead tried to throw up a barrier between himself and God. He tried to use the ship's hull as the barrier in this case. It was a physical wall that made it so Jonah couldn't see or touch or feel what was on the other side. In his mind, what was on the other side was God. However, God was right there next to him the whole time, knowing Jonah's heart and thoughts. He knew that Jonah was afraid. He knew what weighed heavily on his mind. He also knew what it would take to shake up Jonah's mind and heart to remind him of who was in control.

Now, what did God do? Did He send a fly to land on Jonah's nose? Did He send an annoying passenger to sit in the hammock next to him to chew his ear off about life's troubles? No, God sent a storm to beat on that wall. It was a terrible, ferocious storm. Have you ever been in a storm at sea? Imagine for a moment you are in the middle of the ocean with no land in sight. All that you have between you and that cold water is wood boards a few inches thick with a tar-like substance between them. All you can do in trust in the ship's crew. The sailors and the captain of Jonah's ship knew what to do in a normal storm. However, this was no normal storm. The wind and rain and waves would destroy the ship. I can see it in my mind's eye, they were frantically doing all they could to save themselves. They threw as much cargo as they could overboard. Everything they saw as being nonessential to their living through this storm was picked up and thrown into the sea to become lighter and get height over the waves, but with every inch they gained, the waves gained two. After having done everything they could physically do to save themselves they turned to their individual gods for aid. Does this sound like our lives? We get ourselves into overwhelming trouble and try to bail ourselves out, then things just get worse and worse. Then we turn to our worldly gods seeking relief. Things like food, alcohol, drugs of varying forms, TV, physical affection outside of God's given direction on the subject, and others of which I'm sure came to your mind while reading this. No matter which way you look at this subject though, it is a true statement; we want to force things to go our way, on our terms and in our time. Then when things go wrong and don't go according to our grand plans, we try to self soothe and make ourselves feel better. The world wants us to turn to it instead of turning to the One who can really truly help and save us from what is going wrong in life.

Once the crew of the ship saw that their gods weren't able to help they got even more frightened and to look for other answers. Imagine what was going on right now on the deck of this ship. Everyone thinks they will die. Imagine the pandemonium going on inside of their heads when they realize that there is one thing missing from this scene. Or rather, one person missing. They realized that during this whole episode Jonah was still in his cabin and was sleeping through the entire storm. Imagine how you would feel to have done everything you know of to fix a situation only to find out that there was one person who could have possibly fixed it, or helped to fix it, and they were "asleep" and unaware of the situation. The crew went looking for Jonah. They found him in his bunk oblivious to the danger they were in.

How often are we in Jonah's place of being oblivious and unaware of the spiritual danger that those around us are in? Do we walk around asleep or are we throwing up walls and barriers around us to be purposefully unaware of those around us and their problems until we have someone break into our realm and smash through that wall and demand our help in their situation? The crew of this ship were at the end of their rope and had one last choice in their minds and that was to smash through Jonah's wall and get him to help them. They woke him up from what must have been a sound sleep, what else could it have been so he could sleep through this fierce of a storm. The Captain even asked Jonah how he could sleep in the middle of this storm.

The Captain, crew, and I am sure the other passengers implored Jonah to pray for deliverance from the storm and for his God to take pity on them. They were exercising their final option, and that was to turn to the only other one who could, maybe, deliver them from this problem, from their current trial. They tore down every wall and barrier they could and were desperately seeking a way out. How often are we at this point where we finally need to pull down that wall between us and The Lord? We throw that wall up and then He makes us tear it down to have Him help us. We try to hide behind these walls and barriers we create between us and Him. They may not be high walls, more like cubicle height so we can peek over and say "Hi" every once in a while, times like Easter or Christmas, maybe?

However, God knows where you are even while we are running or hiding behind those walls. He sees that next step you are taking whether it is towards Him or away. He can see you taking that bite of ice cream, or in my case of fried chicken, trying to comfort ourselves in the seemingly hopeless situation we are finding ourselves in. He sees it all and while we are stepping around the issue or even stepping away from it; He wants that step to be back towards Him. He wants those walls to come down. He is standing there knocking on that wall wanting to help you in your life in hoping you will ask and allow Him to help.

Are you willing to let God in?

As we read further into the book of Jonah and what he did to hide from God, we see that Jonah goes below deck and goes to sleep. He is trying to shut his troubles and God out of his mind by emptying it and going to sleep.

How often do we try to empty ourselves in relation to those around us? I know that I get to a point in life where I am emotionally done with a certain recurring circumstance and then I give up on trying to solve the issue and then I close myself off from it and empty myself of the issue and try to shift it off to someone else to deal with. That's another form of a barrier that is being thrown up to, at least in our minds, shield us from issues and problems we don't want to see or deal with. Just like Jonah falling asleep on the boat. He didn't want to deal with it. He knew he was shutting out God and what He wanted.

We read further and see what God did. God sent Jonah a reminder of who was really in control. An enormous storm rose around the ship as it was traveling. Yet Jonah remained asleep. How often are we going through a storm in life and yet we remain asleep to the real reason it is there and don't realize Who sent it and why? God sends trials and storms our way for a multitude of reasons. Sometimes it is just to smash through what is standing between us and Him and have us realize that He is truly there for us if we will reach out to Him. When the sailors woke Jonah up and questioned him, he admitted what was going on not only to the crew but also to himself. He recognized the barrier he had put up and the fault it had caused in his life and the problem it had caused in other people's lives.

This was a key moment for him where he began his transition and transformation to become closer to God. God wants us to be close to Him and sometimes He will send something our way to ensure that we know what needs to be happening and how to do that if we will open our eyes and hearts to the message being given. Talk about a hard thing to do. Letting someone into your life and into your heart especially when you have been or believe that person had hurt you before. God will never hurt you intentionally without having a greater purpose in mind. The purpose of the storm and the peril He put Jonah and the ship through was to bring about a great change in Jonah's heart and to bring change and salvation to thousands of other people. Even if it is to save one soul, just your soul, God will give you every opportunity for every soul is precious in His sight.

Jonah saw he needed to save those souls on the ship. He saw it needed action. He saw that he needed to start the process of repentance in the sight of God. He knew that saying "ah shucks, I'm sorry God", would not be enough. So what did Jonah do? He told them to throw him overboard. Talk about a leap of faith. He knew he had messed up and done a severely wrong thing in God's sight and he made sure that the crew knew exactly who it was that sent the storm and that the only way to save themselves was to follow the instructions of God's chosen mouthpiece and servant. They had to follow the Prophet to save themselves. The crew took the leap, overcoming their own barriers and their own belief structure of worshipping false gods and to follow the direction of the Prophet of the one true God. They trusted in their act of following Jonah's instructions to throw him over the side of the ship into the stormy sea. God showed them their faith was not in vain. The storm ceased, and they were safe.

They could finish their journey and you can imagine the change that happened in their lives and hearts. They would not have stayed quiet about what happened to them. They would tell their families, and their friends, and everyone who would listen to them about the events on board their ship that day. This event would allow change and affect many many more people as they hear about what happened on the sea that day. Hundreds if not thousands of people would be positively affected by one person overcoming and breaking down their barrier between them and God.

However, things were not over for Jonah. He still needed more work. How often have we felt that? We were going through a rough patch and we see light at the end of the tunnel and then suddenly that light we saw, that looked like the end of the hard times, was actually the headlight of an oncoming freight train. This is God trying to help us break down more of those walls and barriers we have thrown up to block out Him and anything that might hurt us or that might invade and make our little happy bubble world more like reality.

This is a harsh wake-up call for us. We may come away from the impact with that train feeling like God hates us and all He wants to do is to hurt us. Since sometimes we are the ones being thrown overboard and suddenly feel like as if we are sinking deeper and deeper and unable to find the traction to move forward or to tread water enough to reach that safe harbor we think is where we are supposed to be going to. The point is this, God is in control. He has the plan in his hands for you and He knows where we need to be. As we see in this case with Jonah, God has prepared how he was to go which was not where Jonah thought it would be. That safe harbor for Jonah was not safe and sound on shore. No, it was in the belly of a great fish.

Now the distinction between if it was a fish, or a whale does not really matter. Just try to imagine this event happening. You are sinking into the depths of the sea, and you see this enormous black shadow swimming around getting closer and closer to you. How scared would you be? How many walls between you and God would drop right at that moment when you are fearing for your life, for your existence, for your way of life? What would go through your mind? It might be fear. It might be anger. I think it would probably be feelings of regret and a desire for repentance of his disobedience to God's will and commands. Then right as you can't stand it anymore and are about to give in and let it all end, that black shadowy mass comes along and swallows you whole. You slid down the throat of the beast and down into its belly. You land with a wet plop and realize that you are no longer in the water and are instead surrounded by air and you can breathe. You are safe.

God will give you a safe place to be if you let him past your walls and barriers and fortified barricades. It may not be the most comfortable place, especially if God has to break His way in, however; it will be a safe place. For Jonah, it was safe in the beast's belly but it was definitely not comfortable. This was the stomach of an animal. It was dark; it was foul smelling; it was not where he wanted to be by any stretch of the imagination, but it was safe. There was only one thing that Jonah needed to do to escape from the belly of that beast. He had to rely on God and willingly let Him in. How hard is that to do especially when we are in a hard, difficult time we know was put on us by God? I know from experience it can be hard because of our human nature. God asks us to overcome that carnal human nature and to trust in Him. I know what it is you are thinking. You think it is easier said than done. It can be, that's why you start the process with a little lean.

Think of a time you hurt your ankle, or broke a leg, or did something that made it hard to walk and you needed something outside of you to support yourself. You needed a cane or a crutch or someone to let you use their shoulder. That's what God wants to be for you to get you started on trusting Him and letting God into your life. He will be that shoulder to lean on. He will be that crutch for temporary support. He will be there for you no matter what if you let him. We see Jonah leaning on God through prayer. Jonah prays and asks for forgiveness and shows God that he is opening himself up and breaking down the walls and barricades to let God in. The next part is an important point. How long did it take to accomplish this deed to where God then gets Jonah out of the belly of the beast? It says in chapter 1 of the book of Jonah that he was in there for three days and three nights.

Why do you think they put in this statement of how long Jonah was in the beast's belly? There is a multitude of reasons they state it. It all depends on the study you are doing at the time which shows that God's word speaks to you at the moment and tells you what you need to know. In our case, God's living word is showing us that there was a lesson that Jonah needed to learn and that by extension we also need to learn. That Jonah's release from his uncomfortable situation was not immediate and that it won't be easy or quick for us either. For Jonah, it would not take him saying "Hey God, I'm sorry." And then God responding "Oh ok, we're cool. Let's get you out of there." No, God let him remain in his uncomfortable situation for that amount of time to teach Jonah who was really in control. In your hard and uncomfortable trials when you feel like God is punishing you, that is when it is hardest to let someone in past your protective walls, into your inner sanctum where you feel the most vulnerable, and help you take a step back and see what is really truly going on, however; that is exactly where God wants to be. He is aching to help you see what He is trying to do in your life.

How fantastic is this thought? The one who is putting us into or is allowing us to get ourselves into the uncomfortable, painful, miserable situation wants to come in and help us see why we are there. You would want to fight them and say "no way you can't come in here, look at what you did!" However, think of it this way. For those of us who are parents out there, don't we do the same thing with our kids? We try to protect them when they are young and innocent and to keep them from all bad things. Then there comes the time where we need to let them try that thing that might hurt them and we can't protect them.

As an example, I was teaching my son to ride a bike. He was 4 years old and had mastered so many skills already including riding the bike using his training wheels. Then the time came to let him try to ride without them. He said he was ready, and he showed he was there. So off they came and there he stood, protected the best way I could prepare him to be. He had his helmet, elbow pads, knee pads, and his knowledge of how to do what he was about to do. I had done everything I could. Then as he pedaled, there was only one thing I could do, and that was to let him either succeed or fall in that first attempt. This is the same thing that God does with us. He teaches us, prepares us as best he can with what we allow Him to teach us. He gives us the knee pads and elbow pads and helmet. In fact, he gives us the opportunity to wear a full suit of armor every day of our lives, however; He leaves it up to us to put on and to use that protection and knowledge so we can succeed or fall in our attempt. God will be there by your side to help when He can, but he will let us also feel the pain and uncomfortable feelings of failure when we fall so we can learn that we need to turn back to Him for help just like our children do to us when they fall off that bike.

This is exactly what Jonah did. He broke down the barriers he had hastily thrown up between him and God and he cried out to God for three days and three nights. He turned to and reached out to his Heavenly Father and asked for help, for forgiveness, and for probably a few thousand other things. He knew that he had to allow God in so he could get the help he needed.

Now, what was God's reaction to all of this? Did He yell at Jonah? Did He rant and stomp around berating Jonah for his bad choices in life? Did He ignore His child in need? No. He looked at him in love through the holes in the walls and He reached out wanting to help him in every way he could while still knowing that there was a job for Jonah to do. God sent His help and His love to Jonah in the form of telling that beast to head to shore and to deposit Jonah onto the shoreline. Now the lesson teaching wasn't over at this point. The beast didn't just open its mouth and allow Jonah to walk out onto the shore. No, the animal vomited Jonah onto the shore. Again, those of us who are parents are familiar with the prospect of projectile vomit coming from something, and that's what happened with Jonah.

Now Jonah was free from one situation and I can imagine in my minds eye that once he was on the shore and the beast had left the shore that Jonah went down the shoreline a little ways away from the pool of the stomach contents of the animal he had been inside and then jumped into the water and started to at least rinse the slime and junk from the beast off of him. Yet that was when God came to him and told him once again to go to Nineveh. Jonah was making himself comfortable again when he was "interrupted."

How often have you found yourself in a similar situation? You got out of one rough patch in life and then you are asked, or perhaps pushed, into another. God has a plan and a purpose for all of us, and He wants to help us along that path. Yet He knows that sometimes we need that push. God told Jonah to "Arise, go to Nineveh, that great city, and preach"(Jonah chapter 3 verse 2 NKJV). How great of a command is that? It was the same thing that God told Jonah to do at the beginning of this journey that Jonah tried to hide from. God gave him a great mission to accomplish, yet Jonah hid and run away. He put up as many barricades around himself as possible.

Now that God had come crashing through those barriers, Jonah obeyed and went to Nineveh. This was after God showed Jonah in plain and obvious ways, that what Jonah was doing was not in accordance with God's plan for him. Now take a moment and think about what you are doing in your life that might not be part of God's plan or His will for you. Are you following Him in what He had the prophets write in the Bible for how we are to live our lives in relation to our relationships? To our daily activities? To our finances? To our daily studies and prayer? To our continuous walk with God and trying to bring ourselves closer to Him?

As a Christian, we have already taken one step closer to God, and that is accepting Christ as our Lord and Savior and putting our faith in Him. But is that enough for our daily lives? It is enough to get us into Heaven and to live with Him again, however; we can't be passive believers. In the book of James in the New Testament, it tells us to "be doers of the word, and not hearers only" (James chapter 1 verse 22 NKJV). If we are to be doers of the word, then we are to do what we can to get closer to God every day. The problem arises in when we try to distance ourselves from Him by throwing up those walls and barricades and barriers and creating that virtual minefield to keep everyone and everything out. This then causes problems not only for others who want to get close to us but also for us getting close to anyone at all. Those around us tire of trying to climb over those walls and to navigate the minefield and having those efforts explode around them in failure while they try to get close to if not into the inner sanctum of your life, and they eventually give up and leave or, if they stay, they get so frustrated that they will throw up their own barriers and barricades and walls to keep us out, in fear of being hurt by what your life will do to them while they try to stay by you.

So why would God try to stay by you during this time? Why would God tell His prophet to go tell the people of Nineveh to repent and turn their hearts back to Him and to tear down the walls they had put in place around their hearts? The answer is the same for both questions. God wants to get through your walls and into your life and into your heart for the same reason He sent Jonah to Nineveh. Love. He does these things because He loves you. You, individually and wholly you. He wants you to receive Him and accept Him because He loves you and wants you to live with Him for eternity.

This was God's great message to the people of Nineveh and to us today. Believe in God's word and what he tells us through His messenger. God's message to us today is simple, believe that Christ is your Savior and accept

Him as your Lord and Savior. A simple thing to say, a hard thing to do if you have those walls and barricades in place.

Look at the people of Nineveh. Jonah told them to repent and turn back to God. This was a very evil city. God had them slated for destruction if they did not repent. They had gone so far down the rabbit hole of evil and wickedness that God was ready to push the heavenly button of destruction and wipe that city off the map. But what did they do when presented with God's message through Jonah? They listened, and it convicted them in their hearts and, as we read in chapter 3 of Jonah, from the King down to the lowest of people in the city, they repented. They performed the needed rituals of the time to show that they had changed. They fasted, they prayed, they put on sackcloth and sat in ashes. The King even sent out a decree to everyone in the city that everyone who repented should do these things and he even said the animals should also fast and should be covered in sackcloth and sit in ashes. That is true and whole repentance of the whole city trying to show God that they were turning away from their evil ways and wanted to let Him into their hearts and lives.

How hard would that be for you? Could you sit in the ashes and be uncomfortable and cry to God and allow

Him in? Most people can't imagine doing that, however; remember that what they were doing was putting themselves into an uncomfortable situation purposely and repenting while in that situation. God will put you into that uncomfortable position to push on those walls and hope you take that next step. He hopes it never gets to where he has to do physical reminders of his power in your life. He had to do this for Jonah more than once. He already had him swallowed by a great beast in the sea. But now, after Jonah had delivered his message to Nineveh we see something interesting in chapter 4 of Jonah. We see what happens when we only partially let God in, or we throw up a wall again after something had torn it down.

Jonah's journey of tearing down his own walls hit a stumbling stone when he delivered God's message to Nineveh. Jonah was angry when he saw that people were repenting. He was angry that people were following his message from God and they were allowing God back into their hearts. Jonah was so mad that he prayed and asked God to take his life. Imagine how angry and hurt he was over something he conceived in his own mind and had no basis in factual reality. He was so hurt that he quickly built another wall because he was having an issue accepting that God would give these people a second chance and that they were taking advantage of this chance. Jonah even went out to the east side of the city and built a shelter so he could have a small bit of shade to comfort him while he watched to see what would become of the city.

And while he was sitting there God caused a plant to grow and shade Jonah. And Jonah was happy to have this shade. He was comfortable as he sat and waited for the fireworks of destruction to rain down. So what did God do? He caused a worm to damage the plant overnight. The plant withered, and this also made Jonah angry. Then God reminded him of what was happening. He reminded Jonah that God was in control. He reminded him that the reason He had asked Jonah to deliver this message because it benefited over one hundred thousand people inside those city walls and all the living things around the city.

This was part of what Jonah forgot. That when God wants into our lives, past our walls, past our barricades, through that minefield surrounding us, it's because of His love for us and for what we can, and will do for Him to spread that love to the rest of the people here on Earth that we come into contact with. How awesome and amazing is that? God loves you. He wants you. He needs you to be a tool for His purposes. The question then arises, will you take down those walls and let Him in? Or will you encase them in concrete to fortify them and keep Him out?

Will you come forward and say "Lord here I am. Use me to share your love and your message." Or will you be like the scared, despondent Jonah and run away from God and try to hide? These are some blunt point-blank questions and they can be difficult to answer right away. I have wanted to be a tool in God's hands, but when the time came, I stepped away from the opportunity He gave me. I hid behind my own walls. How often do you feel that way or see yourself behaving that way? How can you overcome it?

How can we be less like the Jonah in the boat's bottom and instead be what God wants you to be? Now we don't want the normal Sunday School answers. We know we should read the Bible, go to church, pray, etc. What else should we do? We need to dive into ourselves and find the foundations of those walls and find out why we put them up so often and so fast. This process will be hard. This process may hurt. In fact, once you poke around inside of yourself, you will probably need help to accomplish this task. You will definitely need the help of God and His Holy Spirit to keep going. You may want to stop, you may feel you need to stop. You may feel you are a failure. You may feel you are failing in points of your life, if not in everything. I felt that way, more than once. Just remember this. Don't stop moving forward on this path. Trust in God, and His love for you. As my Pastor once told me, You cannot out fail God's mercies and grace. He wants you to succeed in this struggle and He wants you to come close to Him in every way of your life just as He wants to be close to you.

Think about that for a moment. While you have been running away and throwing up those walls and barricades and fortifying yourself against anything and everything you can, God has been right there by your side. You have felt that you were pushing him away. You felt as if He had left you. What you had been doing was just keeping everyone else out and turned your spiritual hearing aide down as low as you could. However, God was always there with you right by your side talking to you and holding you up. He loves you with everything he has. He will always love you. And there is only one real true obstacle that can be put between you and that love.

That obstacle is you and how you treat and talk to yourself. Those obstacles and barriers, who do they really end up hurting? You. What do they do to you in your life? They end up tearing you down and making you feel you are of no worth because you don't allow yourself to feel God's love in your life. You allow the negative thoughts and feelings to permeate your life and to block out how God truly feels and thinks about you. This was something that God taught to Jonah when he sent the storm and then the fish and finally the bush.

God will always be there in the storm's midst. From Edge to edge, in the eye, right by your side. The difficult part for us is to let Him in. Through the course of this book so far, I am sure you have seen where you are putting up those walls and you have probably had instances where you have gotten glimpses why those walls have been built around you. However, this is where the most frightening part comes in for most people. This same Person who stands by us at all times in our lives, also asks us for the most difficult thing He can.

He asks us to trust in Him implicitly in everything we do. To give Him our hearts, minds, our whole being. To break down those walls and to let Him in. But how can we do this? How can we even begin the process? Jonah shows us this initial step from while he was in the beast's belly. Remember what he did? He recognized that God was in control and he saw where he had sinned in the past that had brought him to where he was.

Look at your life. Where have you tried to distance yourself from God? Where have you tried to shut other people out? Where are you seeing the areas you need to go to God and start, like Jonah, repenting of past actions? This is the hardest part of breaking down the walls that have been built and fortified for decades. The process will not be easy, nor will it be a short process either. However, with Gods help you can and you will do it, as long as you stick with Him and hold Him close to your side. Seek the counsel of someone who you can trust to hold you to this. With them as your help on this earth and God, your Heavenly Father, as your guide and the best help in this course as you can get.

To conclude this exploratory portion of your journey, I would like to end in this prayer for you my dear reader.

Our Father in heaven. You know all that is in our hearts and in our minds. You know our struggles. You know our pains. You also know our joys and happiness in our lives. Father, you also know the walls we try to used to keep us away from everything we think can or wants to hurt us. Father, we also recognize that through all of this, you continue to love us unconditionally. Now, Father, I ask that you spread that love on the reader of this book as they begin their walk through breaking down those walls that have been built over their lives. I pray that they will feel your love and presence around them as they proceed down this path. Let them feel and

Brian D'Alo

see your guiding hand in their lives as they come closer to you and to others in their lives.

For those that read this book and for myself, I pray for these things in the name of your beloved Son and our Savior, Jesus Christ, Amen.

Printed in the United States
By Bookmasters